Contents

Introduction

Simplicity is the key to many fabulous things, and pizza is no exception.

A crisp, well-cooked pizza base, an aromatic tomato sauce, mozzarella and fragrant basil are the only four elements needed to create the famous Pizza Margherita—one of the joys of Italian cuisine.

Make Me Pizza is packed with 55 fantastically simple pizzas that will make you wonder why you ever ordered take away. From snacks and starters to main events, many, but not all, are based on traditional Italian flavour combinations. In others, ingredients such as broccolini, lentils, pumpkin and lamb make appearances, are all teamed with complementary flavours to form pizzas you'll want to revisit time and time again.

At the back of this book you will find a collection of reliable basics—a great pizza dough, a flavoursome pizza sauce, tapenades and pestos—that are used throughout the book in various recipes. These basics are here both to be used as a starting point for the *Make Me Pizza* recipes and also as building blocks for you to create your own signature pizza creations.

Whether you're looking for pizza that is traditional, contemporary, healthy, vegetarian or one that will cut a few corners to save time, we hope you'll find plenty to tempt you here!

Traditional

Neapolitana pizza

Preparation time: 10 minutes
Cooking time: 12 minutes
Makes: two 30 cm (12 in) square pizzas (serves 4–6)

> 1 quantity pizza dough (see page 118)
> 1 quantity pizza sauce (see page 120)
> 340 g (12 oz/2⅔ cups, loosely packed) coarsely grated mozzarella cheese
> 125 g (4½ oz/1 cup) pitted black olives
> 60 g (2¼ oz/⅓ cup) capers, rinsed, drained
> 16 anchovy fillets, drained on paper towel, halved lengthways

1 Preheat oven to 220°C (425°F/Gas 7). Place two large, heavy baking trays in the oven to heat.

2 Cut the dough into two even portions and shape each into a ball. Press each ball to flatten, then use a lightly floured rolling pin to roll out each ball on a piece of non-stick baking paper to a 30 cm (12 in) square. Spread the pizzas evenly with the pizza sauce, then top with the mozzarella, olives, capers and anchovies.

3 Remove the trays from the oven one at a time to keep them as hot as possible and carefully slide one pizza (still on the baking paper) onto each tray. Bake for 12 minutes, swapping the trays around halfway through cooking, or until the bases are crisp and golden and the mozzarella is bubbling. Serve immediately.

Prosciutto, bocconcini & rocket pizza

Preparation time: 15 minutes
Cooking time: 24 minutes
Makes: four 24 cm (9½ in) round pizzas (serves 4)

2½ tablespoons extra virgin olive oil, plus extra,
   for drizzling
2 garlic cloves, crushed
1 quantity pizza dough (see page 118)
440 g (15½ oz) bocconcini (fresh baby mozzarella cheese),
   drained on paper towel, torn into 2 cm (¾ in) chunks
150 g (5½ oz) thinly sliced prosciutto, roughly torn lengthways
50 g (1¾ oz) rocket (arugula) leaves
125 g (4½ oz/½ cup) olive tapenade (see page 123)

1 Preheat oven to 220°C (425°F/Gas 7). Place two large, heavy pizza or baking trays
in the oven to heat.
2 Combine the olive oil and garlic in a small bowl and stir to combine well. Cut the dough into
four even portions and shape each into a ball. Press each ball to flatten, then use a lightly floured
rolling pin to roll out each ball on a piece of non-stick baking paper to a 24 cm (9½ in) round.
Brush each pizza with some of the garlic oil.
3 Remove the trays from the oven one at a time to keep them as hot as possible and carefully
slide one pizza (still on the baking paper) onto each tray.
4 Bake the pizzas for 8 minutes. Remove the pizzas from the oven and top with half the
bocconcini, scattering evenly. Return the pizzas to the oven, swapping the trays around, and bake
for another 3–4 minutes or until the bocconcini starts to melt and the bases are crisp and golden.
Repeat with the remaining two pizzas and bocconcini.
5 Serve the pizzas immediately, scattered with the prosciutto and rocket, topped with a little of
the tapenade and drizzled with extra olive oil. Serve the remaining tapenade passed separately.

Margherita pizza

Preparation time: 15 minutes
Cooking time: 24 minutes
Makes: four 26 cm (10½ in) round pizzas (serves 4)

 1 quantity pizza dough (see page 118)
 185 ml (6 fl oz/¾ cup) pizza sauce (see page 120)
 150 g (5½ oz) bocconcini (fresh baby mozzarella cheese), thinly sliced
 olive oil, for drizzling
 small basil leaves, to serve

1 Preheat oven to 230°C (450°F/Gas 8). Place two large, heavy pizza or baking trays
in the oven to heat.
2 Cut the dough into four even portions and shape each into a ball. Press each ball to flatten,
then use a lightly floured rolling pin to roll out each ball on a piece of non-stick baking paper to a
26 cm (10½ in) round. Spread the pizzas evenly with the pizza sauce, leaving a small border. Top
with the bocconcini and drizzle with a little olive oil.
3 Remove the trays from the oven one at a time to keep them as hot as possible and carefully
slide one pizza (still on the baking paper) onto each tray. Bake for 10–12 minutes, swapping the
trays around halfway through cooking, or until the bases are crisp and golden. Bake the remaining
two pizzas. Serve immediately, sprinkled with the basil.

Potato & rosemary pizza

Preparation time: 20 minutes
Cooking time: 25–30 minutes
Makes: two 30 cm (12 in) round pizzas (serves 6–8 as a starter)

1 quantity pizza dough (see page 118)
2 tablespoons olive oil
2 garlic cloves, crushed
2 potatoes (such as desiree) (about 300 g/10½ oz), unpeeled, very thinly sliced
1 tablespoon rosemary, plus extra, to serve
1 teaspoon salt

1 Preheat oven to 220°C (425°F/Gas 7).

2 Cut the dough into two even portions and shape each into a ball. Press each ball to flatten, then use a lightly floured rolling pin to roll out each ball on a piece of non-stick baking paper to a 30 cm (12 in) round. Transfer the pizzas (still on the baking paper) to two large, heavy pizza or baking trays.

3 Mix 2 teaspoons of the olive oil with the garlic and brush evenly over the pizzas. Gently toss the remaining olive oil, potato, rosemary, salt and freshly ground black pepper, to taste, in a bowl. Arrange the potato slices in overlapping circles over the pizzas. Drizzle with any oil remaining in the bowl.

4 Bake the pizzas for 25–30 minutes, swapping the trays around halfway through cooking, or until the bases are crisp and golden and the potato is tender. Serve immediately, sprinkled with a little extra rosemary.

Parmesan & rosemary pizza bread

Preparation time: 10 minutes
Cooking time: 16 minutes
Makes: four 24 cm (9½ in) round pizzas (serves 8–12)

> 1 quantity rosemary pizza dough (see page 118)
> 80 ml (2½ fl oz/⅓ cup) extra virgin olive oil
> 50 g (1¾ oz/½ cup, loosely packed) finely shredded parmesan cheese
> sea salt flakes, to serve

1 Preheat oven to 220°C (425°F/Gas 7). Place two large, heavy pizza or baking trays in the oven to heat.
2 Cut the dough into four even portions and shape each into a ball. Press each ball to flatten, then use a lightly floured rolling pin to roll out each ball on a piece of non-stick baking paper to a 24 cm (9½ in) round. Make a border, pressing with your fingertips 2 cm (¾ in) from the edge. Brush the pizzas with the olive oil, sprinkle with the parmesan and season with sea salt.
3 Remove the trays from the oven one at a time to keep them as hot as possible and carefully slide one pizza (still on the baking paper) onto each tray. Bake for 6–8 minutes, swapping the trays around halfway through cooking, or until the bases are crisp and golden. Bake the remaining two pizzas. Serve immediately.

Variations:

Olive pizza bread: After making the borders, brush the pizzas with 2 tablespoons extra virgin olive oil mixed with ½ teaspoon dried oregano. Press 95 g (3¼ oz/½ cup) kalamata olives and 60 g (2¼ oz/⅓ cup) large green olives (remove the pits by placing them on a chopping board and using the heel of your hand to press down so the flesh is in large pieces) into the dough.
Semi-dried tomato & basil pizza bread: After making the borders, brush the pizzas with 2 tablespoons extra virgin olive oil, then lightly press 110 g (3¾ oz/½ cup) semi-dried (sun-blushed) tomatoes into the dough. Season with sea salt flakes. Bake the pizzas for 6 minutes, swapping the trays around halfway through cooking—be careful as the tomatoes can burn easily. Before serving, brush with 2 tablespoons extra virgin olive oil and sprinkle with 3 tablespoons small basil leaves.

Salami pizza bread

Preparation time: 15 minutes
Cooking time: 20 minutes
Makes: four 25 cm (10 in) round pizzas (serves 8–12)

1 quantity pizza dough (see page 118)
160 ml (5¼ fl oz/⅔ cup) pizza sauce (see page 120)
150 g (5½ oz) thinly sliced salami
200 g (7 oz) fresh buffalo mozzarella cheese, thinly sliced

1 Preheat oven to 230°C (450°F/Gas 8). Place two large, heavy pizza or baking trays in the oven to heat.

2 Cut the dough into four even portions and shape each into a ball. Press each ball to flatten, then use a lightly floured rolling pin to roll out each ball on a piece of non-stick baking paper to a 25 cm (10 in) round. Make a border, pressing with your fingertips 2 cm (¾ in) from the edge. Spread the pizzas evenly with the pizza sauce, then top with the salami and mozzarella.

3 Remove the trays from the oven one at a time to keep them as hot as possible and carefully slide one pizza (still on the baking paper) onto each tray. Bake for 10 minutes, swapping the trays around halfway through cooking, or until crisp and golden. Bake the remaining two pizzas. Serve immediately.

Manosha (Arabic pizza)

Preparation time: 15 minutes
Cooking time: 15 minutes
Makes: eight 13 cm (5 in) round pizzas (serves 8 as a snack or starter)

2 tablespoons olive oil, plus extra, for greasing
1 quantity pizza dough (see page 118)
250 g (9 oz) feta cheese, coarsely crumbled
1 teaspoon cumin seeds
1½ teaspoons dried dill or mint
lemon cheeks, to serve

1 Preheat oven to 220°C (425°F/Gas 7). Lightly grease two large, heavy pizza or baking trays with olive oil.

2 Cut the dough into eight even portions and shape each into a ball. Press each ball to flatten, then use a lightly floured rolling pin to roll out each ball on a lightly floured surface to a 13 cm (5 in) round. Place the pizzas on the trays, spacing evenly. Top with the feta, cumin and dill or mint then drizzle with the olive oil.

3 Bake the pizzas for 15 minutes, swapping the trays around halfway through cooking, or until the bases are crisp and golden. Serve immediately or at room temperature, accompanied by the lemon cheeks.

Turkish pizza

Preparation time: 20 minutes (+ cooling time)
Cooking time: 45 minutes
Makes: eight 12 x 18 cm (4½ x 7 in) oval pizzas (serves 8)

60 ml (2 fl oz/¼ cup) olive oil, plus extra, for greasing
1 brown onion, finely chopped
500 g (1 lb 2 oz) minced (ground) lamb
2 garlic cloves, crushed
1 teaspoon ground cinnamon
1½ teaspoons ground cumin
½ teaspoon cayenne pepper
60 g (2¼ oz/¼ cup) tomato paste (concentrated purée)
400 g (14 oz) tin chopped tomatoes
50 g (1¾ oz/⅓ cup) pine nuts
2 tablespoons chopped coriander (cilantro) leaves
1 quantity pizza dough (see page 118)
Greek-style yoghurt, coriander (cilantro) leaves and lemon cheeks, to serve

1 Heat 2 tablespoons of the olive oil in a frying pan over medium–high heat and cook the onion for 5 minutes or until soft but not golden. Add the lamb and cook, breaking up with a wooden spoon, for 10 minutes or until brown. Add the garlic, spices, tomato paste and tomatoes. Cook for 15 minutes, stirring occasionally, until reduced to a thick sauce. Add half the pine nuts and the chopped coriander. Season with salt and freshly ground black pepper. Transfer to a bowl and place in the refrigerator until cooled to room temperature.

2 Preheat oven to 210°C (415°F/Gas 6–7). Lightly grease three large, heavy baking trays with olive oil.

3 Cut the dough into eight even portions and shape each into a ball. Press each ball to flatten, then use a lightly floured rolling pin to roll out each ball on a lightly floured surface to a 12 x 18 cm (4½ x 7 in) oval. Place the pizzas on the trays, spacing evenly. Divide the lamb mixture evenly among the pizzas and spread, leaving a 3 cm (1¼ in) border. Sprinkle with the remaining pine nuts. Brush the edges with a little water. Fold the border up at the edges to contain the filling and then pinch the ends together to form a boat shape. Brush the edges with the remaining olive oil.

4 Bake the pizzas for 15 minutes, swapping the trays around halfway through cooking, or until golden and cooked through. Serve immediately, topped with the yoghurt and coriander, and accompanied by the lemon cheeks.

Mushroom & herb pizza

Preparation time: 20 minutes
Cooking time: 30 minutes
Makes: four 25 cm (10 in) square pizzas (serves 4)

1 tablespoon olive oil
1 large brown onion, cut into thin wedges
2 garlic cloves, sliced
2 x 400 g (14 oz) tins whole tomatoes
1 quantity pizza dough (see page 118)
160 ml (5¼ fl oz/⅔ cup) pizza sauce (see page 120)
250 g (9 oz) fresh buffalo mozzarella cheese, thinly sliced
2 large mushrooms (about 240 g/9 oz), trimmed, peeled,
  cut into 8 mm (⅜ in) slices
⅓ cup chopped flat-leaf (Italian) parsley
¼ cup sage
105 g (3½ oz/½ cup) pesto (see page 122)
80 ml (2½ fl oz/⅓ cup) extra virgin olive oil

1 Heat the olive oil in a large frying pan over medium heat, add the onion and cook, stirring occasionally for 5–6 minutes or until softened. Add the garlic and cook for 1 minute, stirring constantly so the garlic and onion do not take on too much colour. Transfer to a plate to cool.
2 Meanwhile, drain the tinned tomatoes in a colander. Squeeze gently in the palm of your hand to extract most of the seeds and juice. Place on paper towel to absorb excess moisture.
3 Preheat oven to 230°C (450°F/Gas 8). Place two large, heavy baking trays in the oven to heat.
4 Cut the dough into four even portions and shape each into a ball. Press each ball to flatten, then use a lightly floured rolling pin to roll out each ball on a piece of non-stick baking paper to a 25 cm (10 in) square.
5 Spread the pizzas evenly with the pizza sauce, then top with the onion mixture, half the mozzarella, tomatoes, mushroom slices, parsley, sage and then the remaining mozzarella.
6 Remove the trays from oven one at a time to keep them as hot as possible and carefully slide one pizza (still on the baking paper) onto each tray. Bake for 10–12 minutes, swapping the trays around halfway through cooking, or until the bases are crisp and golden. Bake the remaining two pizzas. Combine the pesto and extra virgin olive oil and drizzle over the top of the pizzas. Serve immediately.

Ham, spinach & ricotta calzone

Preparation time: 20 minutes
Cooking time: 20 minutes
Makes: two large calzone (serves 4)

550 g (1 lb 4 oz) firm, fresh ricotta cheese
½ teaspoon freshly grated nutmeg
250 g (9 oz) leg ham, finely chopped
120 g (4¼ oz) finely grated pecorino or parmesan cheese
100g (3½ oz) baby spinach leaves, coarsely chopped
1 quantity pizza dough (see page 118)

1 Combine the ricotta, nutmeg, ham and pecorino or parmesan in a large bowl and season with salt and freshly ground black pepper. Add the spinach and stir to combine.
2 Preheat oven to 220°C (425°F/Gas 7).
3 Cut the dough into two even portions and shape each into a ball. Press each ball to flatten, then use a lightly floured rolling pin to roll out each ball on a piece of non-stick baking paper to a 30 cm (12 in) round. Transfer the dough rounds (still on the baking paper) to two large, heavy baking trays.

4 Divide the ham mixture between the dough rounds, spreading it evenly over one half only and leaving a 1.5 cm (⅝ in) border around the edges. Use a pastry brush or your fingertips to lightly brush the borders with water. Fold the uncovered half of each dough round up and over the filling, then press the edges firmly together in a fluted pattern to seal.
5 Bake for 15–20 minutes, swapping the trays around halfway through cooking, or until golden and cooked through. Serve immediately in slices.

Pepperoni pizza

Preparation time: 15 minutes
Cooking time: 15 minutes
Makes: two 34 cm (13½ in) round pizzas (serves 4)

> 1 quantity pizza dough (see page 118)
> 1 quantity pizza sauce (see page 120)
> 250 g (9 oz) fresh buffalo mozzarella cheese, thinly sliced
> 150 g (5½ oz) pepperoni sausage (see tip), thinly sliced
> 100 g (3½ oz) salami, thinly sliced
> 100 g (3½ oz) thinly sliced pancetta, roughly torn
> mixed leaf salad, to serve

1 Preheat oven to 220°C (425°F/Gas 7). Place two large, heavy pizza or baking trays in the oven to heat.
2 Cut the dough into two even portions and shape each into a ball. Press each ball to flatten, then use a lightly floured rolling pin to roll out each ball on a piece of non-stick baking paper to a 34 cm (13½ in) round. Spread the pizzas evenly with the pizza sauce, then top with the mozzarella, pepperoni, salami and pancetta.
3 Remove the trays from the oven one at a time to keep them as hot as possible and carefully slide one pizza (still on the baking paper) onto each tray. Bake for 15 minutes, swapping the trays around halfway through cooking, or until the bases are crisp and golden and the mozzarella is bubbling. Serve immediately, accompanied by the mixed leaf salad.

TIP: You can replace the pepperoni sausage with 150 g (5½ oz) fresh pork and fennel sausage.

Ham & pineapple pizza

Preparation time: 15 minutes
Cooking time: 20 minutes
Makes: four 25 cm (10 in) round pizzas (serves 4)

1 quantity pizza dough (see page 118)
160 ml (5¼ fl oz/⅔ cup) pizza sauce (see page 120)
320 g (11¼ oz) fresh pineapple, cut into small, thin wedges
200 g (7 oz) leg ham, chopped
125 g (4½ oz/1 cup, loosely packed) coarsely
  grated mozzarella cheese
basil leaves (optional), to serve

1 Preheat oven to 230°C (450°F/Gas 8). Place two large, heavy pizza or baking trays in the oven to heat.
2 Cut the dough into four even portions and shape each into a ball. Press each ball to flatten, then use a lightly floured rolling pin to roll out each ball on a piece of non-stick baking paper to a 25 cm (10 in) round.
3 Spread the pizzas evenly with the pizza sauce, then top with the pineapple, ham and mozzarella.

4 Remove the trays from the oven one at a time to keep them as hot as possible and carefully slide one pizza (still on the baking paper) onto each tray. Bake for 10 minutes, swapping the trays around halfway through cooking, or until the bases are crisp and golden. Bake the remaining two pizzas. Serve immediately, sprinkled with the basil, if using.

Four cheese pizza

Preparation time: 5 minutes
Cooking time: 20 minutes
Makes: four 25 cm (10 in) round pizzas (serves 4)

> 1 quantity pizza dough (see page 118)
> olive oil, for drizzling
> 150 g (5½ oz) bocconcini (fresh baby mozzarella cheese),
>   thinly sliced, drained on paper towel
> 120 g (4¼ oz) firm, fresh ricotta cheese
> 100 g (3½ oz) blue cheese, sliced
> 80 g (2¾ oz) finely grated parmesan cheese

1 Preheat oven to 230°C (450°F/Gas 8). Place two large, heavy pizza or baking trays in the oven to heat.

2 Cut the dough into four even portions and shape each into a ball. Press each ball to flatten, then use a lightly floured rolling pin to roll out each ball on a piece of non-stick baking paper to a 25 cm (10 in) round. Make a border, pressing with your fingertips 2 cm (¾ in) from the edge.

3 Drizzle the pizzas with olive oil and top with the bocconcini. Crumble over the ricotta and blue cheese then sprinkle with the parmesan.

4 Remove the trays from the oven one at a time to keep them as hot as possible and carefully slide one pizza (still on the baking paper) onto each tray. Bake for 10 minutes, swapping the trays around halfway through cooking, until the bases are crisp and golden. Bake the remaining two pizzas. Serve immediately.

Contemporary

Cauliflower & pine nut pizza

Preparation time: 20 minutes
Cooking time: 35–40 minutes
Makes: four 25 cm (10 in) round pizzas (serves 4)

1 tablespoon olive oil
800 g (1 lb 12 oz) cauliflower, cut into small florets
1 quantity parmesan pizza dough (see page 118)
150 g (5½ oz) coarsely grated mozzarella cheese
2 tablespoons currants
50 g (1¾ oz/⅓ cup) pine nuts
70 g (2½ oz/¼ cup) Greek-style yoghurt
1 tablespoon tahini (see tip)
1 tablespoon lemon juice
2 tablespoons chopped flat-leaf (Italian) parsley, to serve

TIP: Tahini is a Middle Eastern paste made from ground sesame seeds. Look for it in the health food section of your supermarket.

1 Heat the olive oil in a large non-stick frying pan over a high heat. Add the cauliflower and cook, stirring occasionally, for 5–6 minutes or until golden and just tender. Remove from the heat and season with salt and freshly ground black pepper.

2 Preheat oven to 230°C (450°F/Gas 8). Place two large, heavy pizza or baking trays in the oven to heat.

3 Cut the dough into four even portions and shape each into a ball. Press each ball to flatten, then use a lightly floured rolling pin to roll out each ball on a piece of non-stick baking paper to a 25 cm (10 in) round.

4 Top the pizzas with half the mozzarella, the cauliflower and currants, then sprinkle with the remaining mozzarella.

5 Remove the trays from the oven one at a time to keep them as hot as possible and carefully slide one pizza (still on the baking paper) onto each tray. Bake for 5 minutes. Remove the pizzas from the oven and sprinkle with half the pine nuts. Return the pizzas to the oven, swapping the trays around, and bake for another 10 minutes, or until the bases are crisp and golden. Repeat with the remaining two pizzas and pine nuts.

6 Meanwhile, combine the yoghurt, tahini and lemon juice in a bowl. Add 1–2 tablespoons of water to thin to the desired consistency.

7 Serve the pizzas immediately, drizzled with the tahini dressing and sprinkled with the parsley.

Ocean trout & zucchini pizza

Preparation time: 20 minutes
Cooking time: 22 minutes
Makes: four 24 cm (9½ in) round pizzas (serves 4)

1 quantity pizza dough (see page 118)
185 g (6½ oz/¾ cup) sour cream
60 g (2¼ oz/¼ cup) firm, fresh ricotta cheese
finely grated zest of 2 lemons
2 zucchini (courgettes), very thinly sliced
  on the diagonal
1 lemon, very thinly sliced
500 g (1 lb 2 oz) skinless ocean trout fillets,
  cut into 3–4 mm (⅛ in) slices

Herb salad
1 tablespoon lemon juice
1½ tablespoons extra virgin olive oil
¼ cup firmly packed dill sprigs
½ cup loosely packed chives snipped into 3 cm
  (1¼ in) lengths
1½ tablespoons baby capers in brine, rinsed, drained

TIP: Try using salmon instead of ocean trout. You can also vary the herbs for the salad—coriander and flat-leaf (Italian) parsley work well.

1 Preheat oven to 230°C (450°F/Gas 8). Place two large, heavy pizza or baking trays in the oven to heat.

2 Cut the dough into four even portions and shape each into a ball. Press each ball to flatten, then use a lightly floured rolling pin to roll out each ball on a piece of non-stick baking paper to a 24 cm (9½ in) round. Make a border, pressing with your fingertips 2 cm (¾ in) from the edge.

3 Combine the sour cream, ricotta, lemon zest and salt and freshly ground black pepper, to taste. Spread a thin layer of the sour cream mixture over each pizza. Top with the zucchini and lemon slices.

4 Remove the trays from the oven one at a time to keep them as hot as possible and carefully slide one pizza (still on the baking paper) onto each tray. Bake for 8 minutes. Remove the pizzas from the oven and top with half the trout slices. Return the pizzas to the oven, swapping the trays around, and bake for another 2–3 minutes or until the bases are crisp and golden. Repeat with the remaining two pizzas and trout.

5 Meanwhile, for the herb salad, combine all the ingredients in a bowl, season with salt and freshly ground black pepper and toss gently. Serve the pizzas immediately, topped with the herb salad.

Spanish pizza bread

Preparation time: 25 minutes (+ cooling time)
Cooking time: 45–50 minutes
Makes: one 25 x 30 cm (10 x 12 in) pizza bread (serves 4–6)

1 tablespoon olive oil, plus extra, for greasing
2 bunches English spinach leaves, washed, drained, shredded
2 brown onions, chopped
2 garlic cloves, crushed
400 g (14 oz) tin whole tomatoes, drained, crushed
¼ teaspoon freshly ground black pepper
1 quantity pizza dough (see page 118)
100 g (3½ oz/⅔ cup) coarsely chopped, pitted black olives

1 Preheat oven to 210°C (415°F/Gas 6–7). Grease a 25 x 30 cm (10 x 12 in) Swiss roll (jelly roll) tin with olive oil.

2 To make the topping, cook the spinach in a large saucepan over low heat, stirring occasionally, for 3–5 minutes or until wilted and the excess water evaporates. Drain the spinach well and set aside to cool. Once cool enough to handle, use your hands to squeeze out any excess moisture from the spinach. Set aside.

3 Heat the oil in the cleaned saucepan over medium–low heat and cook the onion and garlic for 8 minutes or until softened. Add the tomatoes and pepper and simmer gently, stirring occasionally for 5 minutes or until saucy and thickened.

4 Use a lightly floured rolling pin to roll out the pizza dough on a lightly floured surface to the same size as the tin. Place the pizza dough in the tin. Spread the pizza dough with the wilted spinach, top with the tomato mixture and sprinkle with the olives.

5 Bake the pizza bread for 25–30 minutes or until the base is golden and cooked through. Serve warm or at room temperature.

Mini caramelised fennel, fig & prosciutto pizzas with rocket pesto

Preparation time: 20 minutes
Cooking time: 27 minutes
Makes: 15 mini round pizzas

2 teaspoons olive oil
2 fennel bulbs (about 200 g/7 oz each), trimmed,
   thinly sliced
½ teaspoon lemon juice
2 garlic cloves, crushed
1 quantity pizza dough (see page 118)
150 g (5½ oz/¾ cup) rocket pesto (see page 122)
4 firm, ripe figs, sliced lengthways
120 g (4¼ oz) soft goat's cheese, coarsely crumbled
100 g (3½ oz) thinly sliced prosciutto, torn into pieces

1 Heat the olive oil in a large non-stick frying pan over low heat. Add the fennel and lemon juice and cook, stirring occasionally, for 15 minutes or until starting to colour and caramelise. Add the garlic and cook for 2 minutes. Remove from the heat and season with salt and freshly ground black pepper.

2 Preheat oven to 230°C (450°F/Gas 8). Line three large, heavy baking trays with non-stick baking paper.

3 Cut the dough into 15 even portions and shape each into a ball. Press each ball to flatten, then use a lightly floured rolling pin to roll out each ball on a lightly floured surface to a 9 cm (3½ in) round. Place the pizzas on the trays, leaving 3 cm (1¼ in) between each.

4 Spread the pizzas with half the rocket pesto, then top with the caramelised fennel, a fig slice and a little goat's cheese.

5 Bake the pizzas for 10 minutes, swapping the trays around halfway through cooking, or until the bases are crisp and golden.

6 Serve the pizzas immediately, topped with the prosciutto and the remaining pesto.

Ricotta, spinach & bacon pizza pie

Preparation time: 25 minutes
Cooking time: 35 minutes
Makes: one 24 cm (9½ in) pie (serves 6–8)

2 teaspoons olive oil, plus extra, for greasing and brushing
1 large brown onion, chopped
175 g (6 oz) bacon, trimmed of most of the fat, roughly chopped
1 quantity parmesan pizza dough (see page 118)
1 bunch English spinach (about 280 g/10 oz), trimmed, washed, drained
250 g (9 oz) firm, fresh ricotta cheese
¼ cup finely snipped chives
¼ cup lightly packed oregano leaves
finely grated zest of ½ lemon
1 egg
100 g (3½ oz/⅔ cup) crumbled feta cheese
1 quantity roasted tomato pizza sauce (see page 120), to serve

1 Preheat oven to 230°C (450°F/Gas 8). Grease a 24 cm (9½ in) spring-form cake tin with oil.
2 Heat the olive oil in a large frying pan over medium heat and cook the onion and bacon, stirring occasionally, for 5 minutes or until the onion softens. Increase the heat to high and cook for another 1–2 minutes to give a little colour. Transfer to a plate and set aside to cool.
3 Meanwhile, add the spinach to a saucepan of salted boiling water and cook for 1 minute or until just wilted and bright green. Drain and place in iced water to refresh. Drain and then use your hands to squeeze out the water. Place the spinach on a clean tea towel (dish towel) and roll and squeeze to extract any excess moisture. Roughly chop the spinach.
4 Combine the spinach, bacon and onion mixture, ricotta, chives, oregano, lemon zest and egg in a medium bowl. Season with salt and freshly ground black pepper. Mix well to combine. Gently stir through the feta.

5 Shape two-thirds of the dough into a ball. Press to flatten, then use a lightly floured rolling pin to roll out on a lightly floured surface to a 36 cm (14¼ in) round. Shape the remaining dough into a ball and then roll out to a 28 cm (11¼ in) round. Line the base of the tin with the larger round, pressing it into the base and corners and bringing it about 6 cm (2½ in) up the side of the tin. Spoon the filling into the tin and smooth the surface. Brush the rim of the dough lightly with water. Place the remaining round on top. Crimp and fold over the edges to seal. Brush the top with olive oil.
6 Bake for 25 minutes or until golden and cooked through. Cool in the tin for 5 minutes. Serve warm or at room temperature with the pizza sauce.

Chorizo, rosemary, mushroom & rocket pizza

Preparation time: 15 minutes
Cooking time: 20 minutes
Makes: four 25 cm (10 in) round pizzas (serves 2–4)

1 quantity pizza dough (see page 118)
160 g (5¾ oz/⅔ cup) semi-dried tomato tapenade
  (see page 123)
150 g (5½ oz) button mushrooms, thinly sliced
1 chorizo (about 150 g/5½ oz) (see tip), thinly sliced
2 teaspoons chopped rosemary
160 g (5¾ oz) coarsely grated pizza cheese (see tip)
80 g (2¾ oz/2⅓ cups, tightly packed) rocket
  (arugula) leaves
1 tablespoon balsamic vinegar

1 Preheat oven to 220°C (425°F/Gas 7). Place two large, heavy pizza or baking trays in the oven to heat.
2 Cut the dough into four even portions and shape each into a ball. Press each ball to flatten, then use a lightly floured rolling pin to roll out each ball on a piece of non-stick baking paper to a 25 cm (10 in) round. Spread the pizzas with the tapenade, then top with the mushrooms, chorizo, rosemary and pizza cheese.
3 Remove the trays from the oven one at a time to keep them as hot as possible and carefully slide one pizza (still on the baking paper) onto each tray. Bake for 10 minutes, swapping trays halfway through cooking, or until the bases are crisp and golden. Bake the remaining two pizzas.
4 Meanwhile, place the rocket in a medium bowl, drizzle with the balsamic and toss to combine. Serve the pizzas immediately, topped with the dressed rocket.

TIP: You can use thinly sliced pepperoni instead of the chorizo, if you like.

TIP: Pizza cheese is a pre-grated cheese made up of a combination of mozzarella, parmesan and cheddar.

Sardine & silverbeet wholemeal pizza

Preparation time: 20 minutes (+ 10 minutes draining time)
Cooking time: 32 minutes
Makes: two 30 cm (12 in) round pizzas (serves 4)

2½ tablespoons extra virgin olive oil
1 large brown onion, finely chopped
5 garlic cloves, thinly sliced
1 bunch silverbeet (Swiss chard), stems removed,
  leaves washed, dried, coarsely chopped
120 g (4¼ oz/⅔ cup) raisins, coarsely chopped
150 g (5½ oz/1½ cups, loosely packed)
  finely shredded parmesan cheese
large pinch of chilli flakes, or to taste
1 quantity wholemeal pizza dough (see page 118)
2 x 106 g (3½ oz) tins sardines in oil, drained, halved lengthways
finely grated parmesan cheese (optional), to serve

1 Heat the oil in a large saucepan over medium–high heat and cook the onion for 6–8 minutes, or until soft and starting to colour. Add the garlic and cook for 30 seconds or until aromatic. Add the silverbeet and raisins, cover, then cook for 3 minutes, stirring often, or until the silverbeet wilts. Transfer the mixture to a colander and set aside for 10 minutes to drain. Use your hands to squeeze out excess moisture then place in a bowl. Stir in the parmesan, chilli, and salt and freshly ground black pepper.

2 Preheat oven to 220°C (425°F/Gas 7). Place two large, heavy pizza or baking trays in the oven to heat.

3 Cut the dough into two even portions and shape each into a ball. Press each ball to flatten, then use a lightly floured rolling pin to roll out each ball on a piece of non-stick baking paper to a 30 cm (12 in) round. Divide the silverbeet mixture between the bases, scattering to cover, then arrange the sardines on top.

4 Remove the trays from the oven one at a time to keep them as hot as possible and carefully slide one pizza (still on the baking paper) onto each tray. Bake the pizzas for 18–20 minutes, swapping the trays around halfway through cooking, or until the bases are crisp and golden. Serve immediately, sprinkled with the parmesan, if using.

Chilli vongole pizza

Preparation time: 10 minutes
Cooking time: 25 minutes
Makes: four 24 cm (9½ in) round pizzas (serves 4)

1 kg (2 lb 4 oz) clams (vongole), washed
1 quantity pizza dough (see page 118)
1 quantity tomato & chilli pizza sauce (see page 120)
200 g (7 oz) bocconcini (fresh baby mozzarella cheese),
    thinly sliced, drained on paper towel
2 garlic cloves, thinly sliced
2 tablespoons chopped flat-leaf (Italian) parsley
finely grated zest of 1 lemon
1 tablespoon extra virgin olive oil

1 Place the clams in a large, deep frying pan or saucepan over medium heat with 1.5 cm (⅝ in) of water. Bring to a simmer and remove the clams with tongs as they open. Discard any unopened clams. Remove half the clams completely from their shells. (If you are using larger clams, leave the other half in their shells but remove the top shell.) Set aside to cool.

2 Preheat oven to 230°C (450°F/Gas 8). Place two large, heavy pizza or baking trays in the oven to heat.

3 Cut the dough into four even portions and shape each into a ball. Press each ball to flatten, then use a lightly floured rolling pin to roll out each ball on a piece of non-stick baking paper to a 24 cm (9½ in) round. Spread the pizzas evenly with the pizza sauce, then top with half the bocconcini, the garlic, parsley and lemon zest. Top with the remaining bocconcini. Drizzle with the extra virgin olive oil and season with salt and freshly ground black pepper.

4 Remove the trays from the oven one at a time to keep them as hot as possible and carefully slide one pizza (still on the baking paper) onto each tray. Bake for 7 minutes. Remove the pizzas from the oven and top with half the shelled and unshelled clams. Return the pizzas to the oven, swapping the trays around, and bake for another 3–4 minutes, or until the bases are crisp and golden. Repeat with the remaining two pizzas and clams. Serve immediately.

Chicken & parmesan gremolata pizza

Preparation time: 15 minutes
Cooking time: 25 minutes
Makes: four 23 cm (9 in) square pizzas (serves 4)

400 g (14 oz) boneless, skinless chicken breasts, cut across
   the grain, thinly sliced
4 garlic cloves, finely chopped
finely grated zest of 2 lemons
½ cup finely chopped flat-leaf (Italian) parsley
70 g (2½ oz/½ cup) finely grated parmesan cheese
1 quantity pizza dough (see page 118)
1 quantity pizza sauce (see page 120)
280 g (10 oz) fresh buffalo mozzarella cheese, thinly sliced
120 g (4¼ oz/½ cup) whole-egg mayonnaise

1 Preheat oven to 230°C (450°F/Gas 8). Place two large, heavy baking trays in the oven to heat.

2 Combine the chicken, garlic, lemon zest, parsley, parmesan and salt and freshly ground black pepper, to taste, in a bowl and stir well to coat the chicken.

3 Cut the dough into four even portions and shape each into a ball. Press each ball to flatten, then use a lightly floured rolling pin to roll out each ball on a piece of non-stick baking paper to a 23 cm (9 in) square. Make a border, pressing with your fingertips 2 cm (¾ in) from the edge.

4 Spread the pizzas with the pizza sauce, top with the mozzarella and then top with the chicken mixture.

5 Remove the trays from the oven one at a time to keep them as hot as possible and carefully slide one pizza (still on the baking paper) onto each tray. Bake for 10–12 minutes, swapping the trays around halfway through cooking, or until the bases are crisp and golden. Bake the remaining two pizzas.

6 Meanwhile, thin the mayonnaise with a little water. Serve the pizzas immediately, drizzled with the mayonnaise.

Haloumi, chilli, prawn & cherry tomato pizza

Preparation time: 20 minutes
Cooking time: 16 minutes
Makes: two 20 x 35 cm (8 x 14 in) rectangle pizzas (serves 4)

2 tablespoons olive oil
200 g (7 oz) haloumi cheese, thinly sliced
1 quantity pizza dough (see page 118), made using
  2 tablespoons finely chopped oregano when
  adding the olive oil
800 g (1 lb 12 oz) raw prawns (shrimp),
  peeled, deveined, tails left intact
125 ml (4 fl oz/½ cup) tomato & chilli pizza sauce (see page 120)
250 g (9 oz) cherry tomatoes, halved
oregano leaves, to serve

1 Preheat oven to 230°C (450°F/Gas 8). Place two large, heavy baking trays in the oven to heat.
2 Heat 1 tablespoon of the olive oil in a large frying pan over medium–high heat until hot. Add half the haloumi and cook for 2–3 minutes, turning once, or until golden. Remove from the pan and repeat with the remaining haloumi. Set aside.
3 Cut the dough into two even portions and shape each into a ball. Press each ball to flatten, then use a lightly floured rolling pin to roll out each ball on a piece of non-stick baking paper to a 20 x 35 cm (8 x 14 in) rectangle.
4 Toss the prawns with the remaining olive oil. Spread the bases with the pizza sauce, then top with the tomatoes, prawns and haloumi.
5 Remove the trays from the oven one at a time to keep them as hot as possible and carefully slide one pizza (still on the baking paper) onto each tray. Bake for 10 minutes, swapping the trays around halfway through cooking, or until the bases are golden and crisp. Serve immediately, sprinkled with the oregano.

Individual salami & ham calzone

Preparation time: 20 minutes
Cooking time: 12–15 minutes
Makes: four calzone (serves 4)

1 quantity wholemeal pizza dough (see page 118)
125 ml (4 fl oz/½ cup) pizza sauce (see page 120)
160 g (5¾ oz/1¼ cups, loosely packed) coarsely grated mozzarella cheese
100 g (3½ oz) piece of salami, cut into 1 cm (½ in) cubes
100 g (3½ oz) leg ham, chopped
4 eggs, lightly beaten
1 tablespoon chopped flat-leaf (Italian) parsley
100 g (3½ oz) firm, fresh ricotta cheese
2 teaspoons olive oil
2 tablespoons finely shredded parmesan cheese

1 Preheat oven to 230°C (450°F/Gas 8). Place two large, heavy pizza or baking trays in the oven to heat.

2 Cut the dough into four even portions and shape each into a ball. Press each ball to flatten, then use a lightly floured rolling pin to roll out each ball on a piece of non-stick baking paper to a 25 cm (10 in) round.

3 Spread the dough rounds evenly with the pizza sauce. Place the mozzarella, salami and ham in a bowl, add the egg, parsley and salt and freshly ground black pepper, to taste, and stir to combine. Break the ricotta into large pieces over the top and gently stir to combine.

4 Divide the salami mixture among the dough rounds, piling it evenly over one half only. Use a pastry brush to lightly brush the borders with the olive oil. Fold the uncovered half of each dough round up and over the filling, then press the edges together to seal well.

5 Remove the trays from the oven one at a time to keep them as hot as possible and carefully slide two calzone (still on the baking paper) onto each tray. Sprinkle the tops of the calzone with the parmesan. Bake for 12–15 minutes, swapping the trays around halfway through cooking, or until the dough is crisp and golden. Cool for 2–3 minutes before serving.

Broccolini chilli pizza

Preparation time: 15 minutes
Cooking time: 16 minutes
Makes: two 30 cm (12 in) round pizzas (serves 2–4)

150 g (5½ oz) soft goat's cheese or goat's curd,
broken into large chunks
70g (2½ oz/⅓ cup) finely grated
Parmigiano Reggiano or parmesan cheese
80 ml (2½ fl oz/⅓ cup) extra virgin olive oil
3 small red chillies, thinly sliced on the diagonal
4 garlic cloves, thinly sliced
2 bunches broccolini (see tip), trimmed, halved lengthways
1 quantity pizza dough (see page 118)
12 anchovy fillets, drained on paper towel, halved
lengthways

> **TIP:** Use 400g (14 oz) small broccoli florets instead of broccolini, if you like.

1 Preheat oven to 220°C (425°F/Gas 7). Place two large, heavy pizza or baking trays in the oven to heat.
2 Combine the goat's cheese, parmesan and salt and freshly ground black pepper, to taste.
3 Place the olive oil, chilli and garlic in a small saucepan and cook over low heat for 3 minutes or until the garlic just turns golden. Remove from the heat and set aside.
4 Cook the broccolini in a saucepan of boiling water for 1 minute or until tender crisp and bright green. Drain and rinse under cold water to refresh. Pat dry with paper towel.
5 Cut the dough into two even portions and shape each into a ball. Press each ball to flatten, then use a lightly floured rolling pin to roll out each ball on a piece of non-stick baking paper to a 30 cm (12 in) round.
6 Top the pizzas with the cheese mixture, anchovies and broccolini.
7 Remove the trays from the oven one at a time to keep them as hot as possible and carefully slide one pizza (still on the baking paper) onto each tray. Bake for 10–12 minutes, swapping the trays around halfway through cooking, or until the bases are golden and crisp.
8 Serve immediately, drizzled with the chilli and garlic oil and sprinkled with freshly ground black pepper, if desired.

Lamb & rosemary pizza

Preparation time: 10 minutes
Cooking time: 28 minutes
Makes: four 25 cm (10 in) round pizzas (serves 4)

olive oil, for brushing
300 g (10 oz) haloumi cheese, thinly sliced
1 quantity rosemary pizza dough (see page 118)
1 quantity semi-dried tomato tapenade (see page 123)
500 g (1 lb 2 oz) lamb leg steaks (1 cm/½ in thick)
1 quantity mint & chilli pesto (see page 122)
¼ cup firmly packed flat-leaf (Italian) parsley leaves
lemon wedges, to serve

1 Preheat oven to 230°C (425°F/Gas 7). Place two large, heavy pizza or baking trays in the oven to heat.
2 Brush a chargrill pan with olive oil and heat over medium–high heat. Add the haloumi and cook for 1–2 minutes or until golden on one side.
3 Cut the dough into four even portions and shape each into a ball. Press each ball to flatten, then use a lightly floured rolling pin to roll out each ball on a piece of non-stick baking paper to a 25 cm (10 in) round.
4 Spread the tapenade over the pizzas, then top with the haloumi, charred sides up.
5 Remove the trays from the oven one at a time to keep them as hot as possible and carefully slide one pizza (still on the baking paper) onto each tray. Bake for 12 minutes, swapping the trays around after 5 minutes, or until the bases are golden and crisp. Bake the remaining two pizzas.
6 Meanwhile, rub the lamb with half the pesto. Brush a chargrill pan with olive oil and heat over high heat. Add the lamb and cook for about 1 minute each side for rare, or until cooked to your liking. Transfer the lamb to a chopping board and set aside for 5 minutes to rest. Cut the lamb across the grain into 5 mm (¼ in) slices.
7 Serve the pizzas immediately, topped with the chargrilled lamb, remaining pesto and parsley leaves, and accompanied by the lemon wedges.

Chorizo pizza rolls

Preparation time: 20 minutes (+ plus cooling time)
Cooking time: 40 minutes
Makes: ten rolls (serves 10)

2½ tablespoons olive oil
2 brown onions, halved, thinly sliced
2 chorizo (about 300 g/10½ oz), cut into 1.5 cm (⅝ in) chunks
1 quantity pizza dough (see page 118)
125 ml (4 fl oz/½ cup) roasted tomato pizza sauce (see page 120)
120 g (4¼ oz/1 cup) coarsely grated parmesan cheese

1 Heat 2 tablespoons of the olive oil in a large frying pan over medium heat and cook the onion, stirring occasionally, for 10 minutes or until softened. Add the chorizo and cook for another 10 minutes, stirring occasionally (the onion will start to caramelise so you need to keep it moving so it doesn't burn). Transfer to a plate and set aside to cool.

2 Preheat oven to 200°C (400°F/Gas 6). Line two large, heavy baking trays with non-stick baking paper.

3 Shape the dough into a ball. Press the dough to flatten, then use a lightly floured rolling pin to roll out the dough on a lightly floured surface to a 30 x 45 cm (12 x 17¾ in) rectangle.

4 With the longest side closest to you, spread the dough evenly with the pizza sauce, leaving a 5 cm (2 in) border at the edge furthest from you and a 1 cm (½ in) border along the remaining three sides. Brush the border with the remaining olive oil. Top the sauce with the cooled onion and chorizo mixture and half the parmesan.

5 Starting with the edge closest to you, roll up the dough into a log. Cut the log into 10 even portions, wiping the knife clean after each cut. Place five scrolls, cut sides up, on each tray, spacing evenly. Sprinkle the scrolls with the remaining parmesan and then press each to flatten slightly to about 3 cm (1¼ in) thick.

6 Bake for 20 minutes, swapping the trays around halfway through cooking, or until golden and cooked through. Serve warm.

Pear, prosciutto, blue cheese & walnut pizza

Preparation time: 20 minutes
Cooking time: 20 minutes
Makes: two 25 cm (10 in) round pizzas (serves 4 as a starter)

1 tablespoon olive oil, plus extra, for drizzling
2 large, firm, ripe pears (such as williams)
  (about 700 g/1 lb 9 oz), peeled, cored, thinly sliced
½ quantity pizza dough (see page 118)
65 g (2½ oz/½ cup, loosely packed) coarsely grated
  mozzarella cheese
75 g (2¾ oz) blue cheese, crumbled
60 g (2¼ oz/½ cup) walnut halves, coarsely chopped
60 g (2¼ oz) thinly sliced prosciutto, torn into large pieces
60 g (2¼ oz/1⅔ cups tightly packed) rocket (arugula)

1 Heat the olive oil in a large non-stick frying pan over high heat. Add the pears and cook, shaking the pan and flipping them over occasionally, for 5 minutes or until lightly golden.

2 Preheat oven to 220°C (425°F/Gas 7). Place two large, heavy pizza or baking trays in the oven to heat.

3 Cut the dough into two even portions and shape each into a ball. Press each ball to flatten, then use a lightly floured rolling pin to roll out each ball on a piece of non-stick baking paper to a 25 cm (10 in) round.

4 Sprinkle the pizzas with the mozzarella, then top with the pears.

5 Remove the trays from the oven one at a time to keep them as hot as possible and carefully slide one pizza (still on the baking paper) onto each tray. Bake for 6 minutes. Remove the pizzas from the oven and top with the blue cheese and walnuts. Return the pizzas to the oven, swapping the trays around, and bake for another 6–8 minutes or until the bases are golden and crisp.

6 Top the pizzas with the prosciutto, rocket and some freshly ground black pepper, to taste. Serve immediately, drizzled with a little extra olive oil.

Healthy

Chargrilled zucchini, mint & ricotta pizza

Preparation time: 10 minutes
Cooking time: 15 minutes
Makes: two 20 x 35 cm (8 x 14 in) rectangle pizzas (serves 4)

1 quantity pizza dough (see page 118)
olive oil spray
2 large zucchini (courgettes), trimmed,
  cut into 5 mm (¼ in) slices on the diagonal
1 quantity reduced-fat mint & chilli pesto (see tips)
2 teaspoons finely grated lemon zest
165 g (5¾ oz/⅔ cup) firm, fresh low-fat ricotta cheese,
  broken into chunks
small mint leaves, to serve

1 Preheat oven to 230°C (450°F/Gas 8). Place two large, heavy pizza or baking trays in the oven to heat.

2 Cut the dough into two even portions and shape each into a ball. Press each ball to flatten, then use a lightly floured rolling pin to roll out each ball on a piece of non-stick baking paper to a 20 x 35 cm (8 x 14 in) rectangle.

3 Heat a chargrill pan over high heat and spray with the olive oil spray. Grill the zucchini for 2–3 minutes each side or until lightly charred and tender. Spread the pizzas evenly with the pesto, then top with the zucchini, lemon zest and ricotta chunks.

4 Remove the trays from the oven one at a time to keep them as hot as possible and carefully slide one pizza (still on the baking paper) onto each tray. Bake for 10 minutes, swapping the trays around halfway through cooking, or until the bases are crisp and golden. Serve immediately, sprinkled with the mint.

TIP: This pizza is ideal to serve as party fare. Simply cut the pizza into small squares or fingers.

TIP: Follow the pesto recipe on page 122 but reduce the parmesan to 25 g (1 oz), omit the pine nuts, reduce the olive oil to 1 tablespoon and add 2½ tablespoons water with the oil.

Seafood pizza with dill, asparagus & lemon

Preparation time: 30 minutes
Cooking time: 24 minutes
Makes: four 25 cm (10 in) round pizzas (serves 4)

1 quantity basic pizza dough (see page 118)
3 tablespoons finely chopped dill,
  plus extra sprigs, to garnish
160 ml (5¼ fl oz/⅔ cup) roasted tomato
  pizza sauce (see page 120)
105 g (3½ oz/¾ cup, loosely packed) coarsely grated
  low-fat mozzarella cheese
2 bunches asparagus, trimmed, halved
350 g (12 oz) raw prawns (shrimp), peeled,
  deveined, tails left intact
16 scallops, roe removed
250 g (9 oz) squid rings
300 g (10½ oz) skinless firm white fish fillets,
  cut into 2 cm (¾ in) chunks
95 g (3¼ oz/⅓ cup) low-fat plain yoghurt
1 tablespoon lemon juice
lemon wedges, to serve

> **TIP:** Any combination of seafood can be used for this pizza. It is best to avoid frozen seafood, however, as excess water will prevent the pizza from becoming crisp.

1 Preheat oven to 230°C (450°F/Gas 8). Place two large, heavy pizza or baking trays in the oven to heat.
2 Knead 2 tablespoons of the dill into the dough. Cut the dough into four even portions and shape each into a ball. Press each ball to flatten, then use a lightly floured rolling pin to roll out each ball on a piece of non-stick baking paper to a 25 cm (10 in) round. Make a border, pressing with your fingertips 2 cm (¾ in) from the edge.
3 Spread each pizza with the pizza sauce, then top with the mozzarella and asparagus.
4 Remove the trays from the oven one at a time to keep them as hot as possible and carefully slide one pizza (still on the baking paper) onto each tray. Bake for 6 minutes. Remove the pizzas from the oven and top with half the prawns, scallops, squid and fish. Return the pizzas to the oven, swapping the trays around, and bake for another 6 minutes or until the bases are crisp and golden and the seafood is just cooked. Repeat with the remaining two pizzas and seafood.
5 Meanwhile, combine the yoghurt, lemon juice and the remaining chopped dill. Serve the pizzas immediately, drizzled with a little of the yoghurt mixture, garnished with the dill sprigs and accompanied by the lemon wedges.

Mushroom, ricotta & olive pizza pie

Preparation time: 20 minutes (+ cooling time)
Cooking time: 55 minutes
Makes: one pie (serves 6–8)

4 roma (plum) tomatoes, quartered
½ teaspoon sugar
2 teaspoons olive oil
2 garlic cloves, crushed
1 brown onion, thinly sliced
750 g (1 lb 10 oz) mushroom caps, trimmed, sliced
1 quantity pizza dough (see page 118)
250 g (9 oz) firm, fresh low-fat ricotta cheese
2 tablespoons sliced black olives
¼ cup basil leaves, to serve

1 Preheat oven to 210°C (415°F/Gas 6–7). Line a baking tray with non-stick baking paper.
2 Place the tomato quarters on the lined tray and sprinkle with the sugar, and salt and freshly ground black pepper. Roast the tomato for 20 minutes or until the edges start to darken.
3 Meanwhile, heat the oil in a large frying pan over medium heat and cook the garlic and onion for 8 minutes or until soft. Increase the heat to medium–high, add half the mushrooms and cook, stirring occasionally, until they are tender and all the liquid has evaporated. Transfer to a bowl. Repeat with the remaining mushrooms. Set aside to cool.

4 Shape the dough into a ball and press to flatten. Use a lightly floured rolling pin to roll out the dough on a 40 cm (16 in) square piece of non-stick baking paper to a 38 cm (15 in) round. Slide the pizza (still on the baking paper) onto a large, heavy baking tray. Spread with the ricotta, leaving a 5 cm (2 in) border. Top with the mushrooms, tomatoes and olives. Fold the dough edge over the filling to form a border, folding to fit.
5 Bake for 25 minutes or until the pizza crust is golden and cooked through. Serve immediately, sprinkled with the basil.

Spinach, grape & rosemary pizza with cornmeal crust

Preparation time: 15 minutes
Cooking time: 20 minutes
Makes: four 16 x 25 cm (6¼ x 10 in) rectangle pizzas (serves 4)

>   1 quantity pizza dough (see page 118), made using
>   100 g (3½ oz) cornmeal instead of 100 g
>   (3½ oz/⅔ cup) of the plain flour
>   125 g (4½ oz/½ cup) light sour cream
>   120 g (4¼ oz) firm, fresh low-fat ricotta cheese
>   2 tablespoons chopped rosemary
>   100 g (3½ oz) baby spinach leaves
>   300 g (10½ oz) small, seedless black grapes
>   50 g (1¾ oz/⅓ cup) pine nuts
>   2 teaspoons extra virgin olive oil
>   2 teaspoons white wine vinegar

1 Preheat oven to 230°C (450°F/Gas 8). Place two large, heavy baking trays in the oven to heat.

2 Cut the dough into four even portions and shape each into a ball. Press each ball to flatten, then use a lightly floured rolling pin to roll out each ball on a piece of non-stick baking paper to a 16 x 25 cm (6¼ x 10 in) rectangle. Make a border, pressing with your fingertips 2 cm (¾ in) from the edge.

3 Combine the sour cream, ricotta, rosemary and salt and freshly ground black pepper, to taste. Spread the sour cream mixture over the pizzas, leaving a small border around the edge, then top with the spinach and grapes.

4 Remove the trays from the oven one at a time to keep them as hot as possible and carefully slide one pizza (still on the baking paper) onto each tray. Bake for 5 minutes. Remove the pizzas from the oven and sprinkle with half the pine nuts. Return the pizzas to the oven, swapping the trays around, and bake for another 5 minutes or until the bases are crisp and golden. Repeat with the remaining two pizzas and pine nuts.

5 Serve the pizzas immediately, brushed with the combined oil and vinegar and sprinkled with freshly ground black pepper, if desired.

Pumpkin & ricotta pizza

Preparation time: 20 minutes
Cooking time: 40 minutes
Makes: four 23 cm (9 in) square pizzas (serves 4)

> 700 g (1 lb 9 oz) butternut pumpkin (squash),
>   halved lengthways, cut into 5 mm (¼ in) slices
> 1 garlic bulb, divided into cloves, unpeeled
> 2 tablespoons olive oil
> 1 quantity pizza dough (see page 118)
> 230 g (8 oz/1 cup) firm, fresh low-fat ricotta cheese,
>   broken into large chunks
> 140 g (5 oz/1 cup) frozen peas
> ⅓ cup small sage leaves, to serve

1 Preheat oven to 200°C (400°F/Gas 6). Place the pumpkin, garlic cloves and olive oil in a bowl and toss to combine. Spread on a baking tray and roast for 20 minutes or until the pumpkin and garlic are soft. Allow to cool slightly and when cool enough to handle, remove the skins from the garlic cloves.

2 Meanwhile, increase oven to 230°C (450°F/Gas 8). Place two large, heavy baking trays in the oven to heat.

3 Cut the dough into four even portions and shape each into a ball. Press each ball to flatten, then use a lightly floured rolling pin to roll out each ball on a piece of non-stick baking paper to a 23 cm (9 in) square. Make a border, pressing with your fingertips 2 cm (¾ in) from the edge.

4 Top the pizzas with the ricotta chunks, peas, pumpkin, garlic and salt and freshly ground black pepper, to taste.

5 Remove the trays from the oven one at a time to keep them as hot as possible and carefully slide one pizza (still on the baking paper) onto each tray. Bake for 10 minutes, swapping the trays around halfway through cooking, or until the bases are golden and crisp. Bake the remaining two pizzas. Serve the pizzas immediately, sprinkled with the sage.

Mushroom, spinach, oregano & goat's curd pizza

Preparation time: 20 minutes
Cooking time: 26 minutes
Makes: four 25 cm (10 in) round pizzas (serves 4)

olive oil spray
200 g (7 oz) Swiss brown mushrooms, sliced
150 g (5½ oz) oyster mushrooms, sliced
2 garlic cloves, crushed
250 g (9 oz) baby spinach leaves
1 quantity wholemeal pizza dough (see page 118)
2 tablespoons chopped oregano
120 g (4¼ oz) goat's curd (see tip), broken into chunks

TIP: The goat's curd can be replaced with low-fat ricotta cheese or soft goat's cheese. Any combination of mushrooms can be used, such as shiitake, button, enoki, etc.

1 Heat a large non-stick frying pan over high heat and spray with the olive oil spray. Add the mushrooms and cook, stirring, for 3–4 minutes or until golden. Add the garlic and spinach and cook for another 2 minutes or until the spinach is just wilted.

2 Preheat oven to 230°C (450°F/Gas 8). Place two large, heavy pizza or baking trays in the oven to heat.

3 Cut the dough into four even portions and shape each into a ball. Press each ball to flatten, then use a lightly floured rolling pin to roll out each ball on a piece of non-stick baking paper to a 25 cm (10 in) round. Make a border, pressing with your fingertips 2 cm (¾ in) from the edge.

4 Spread the mushroom mixture evenly over the pizzas, then top with the oregano and goat's curd.

5 Remove the trays from the oven one at a time to keep them as hot as possible and carefully slide one pizza (still on the baking paper) onto each tray. Bake for 10 minutes, swapping the trays around halfway through cooking, or until the bases are crisp and golden. Bake the remaining two pizzas. Serve immediately.

Smoked salmon pizzas

Preparation time: 15 minutes
Cooking time: 15 minutes
Makes: six small oval pizzas (serves 6)

6 small oval pitta breads
230 g (8 oz/1 cup) firm, fresh low-fat ricotta cheese
1 small red onion, thinly sliced
1 tablespoon baby capers, rinsed, drained
125 g (4½ oz) smoked salmon slices
dill sprigs, to serve
lemon wedges, to serve

1 Preheat oven to 180°C (350°F/Gas 4). Line two baking trays with non-stick baking paper.
2 Place the pitta breads on the trays. Place the ricotta in a bowl, season with salt and freshly ground black pepper and stir to combine. Spread the ricotta over the pitta breads, leaving a small border around the edges. Top with the onion and capers.
3 Bake the pizzas for 15 minutes, swapping the trays around halfway through cooking, or until the bases are crisp around the edges.
4 Serve immediately, topped with the smoked salmon and dill and seasoned with freshly ground black pepper, to taste, if desired. Accompany with the lemon wedges.

Moroccan chicken pizza

Preparation time: 25 minutes
Cooking time: 30 minutes
Makes: four 24 cm (9½ in) round pizzas (serves 4)

1 teaspoon ground cumin
1 teaspoon ground coriander
½ teaspoon ground cinnamon
400 g (14 oz) boneless, skinless chicken breasts, thinly sliced
olive oil spray
1 large red onion, thinly sliced
200 g (7 oz) baby spinach leaves
1 tablespoon currants
1 quantity pizza dough (see page 118)
160 ml (5¼ fl oz/⅔ cup) pizza sauce (see page 120)
90 g (3¼ oz/⅔ cup, loosely packed) coarsely grated
  low-fat mozzarella cheese
½ cup flat-leaf (Italian) parsley leaves
½ preserved lemon, or to taste, flesh and white pith
  removed, thinly sliced (see tip)

TIP: Preserved lemon is available from the condiment section of larger supermarkets and delicatessens. If you can't find it, you can replace it with the zest of ½ lemon, white pith removed, and very thinly sliced.

1 Combine the cumin, coriander and cinnamon. Toss the chicken in the spice mixture to coat evenly. Heat a large non-stick frying pan over high heat and spray with the olive oil spray. Cook the onion, stirring occasionally, for 3–4 minutes or until golden. Add the chicken and cook, stirring occasionally, for another 3–4 minutes or until lightly golden. Add the spinach and currants and cook for another 1 minute or until the spinach is just wilted. Remove from the heat.

2 Preheat oven to 230°C (450°F/Gas 8). Place two large, heavy pizza or baking trays in the oven to heat.

3 Cut the dough into four even portions and shape each into a ball. Press each ball to flatten, then use a lightly floured rolling pin to roll out each ball on a piece of non-stick baking paper to a 24 cm (9½ in) round. Make a border, pressing with your fingertips 2 cm (¾ in) from the edge.

4 Spread the pizzas evenly with the pizza sauce, then top with the chicken and spinach mixture. Sprinkle with the mozzarella.

5 Remove the trays from the oven one at a time to keep them as hot as possible and carefully slide one pizza (still on the baking paper) onto each tray. Bake for 10 minutes, swapping the trays around halfway through cooking, or until the bases are golden and crisp. Bake the remaining two pizzas.

6 Meanwhile, combine the parsley and preserved lemon. Serve the pizzas immediately, topped with the parsley salad.

Tomato, chicken & broccoli pizza

Preparation time: 20 minutes
Cooking time: 22 minutes
Makes: four 25 cm (10 in) round pizzas (serves 4)

350 g (12 oz) broccoli, trimmed, cut
  into small florets
1 quantity pizza dough (see page 118)
90 g (3¼ oz/⅓ cup) tomato paste (concentrated purée)
300 g (10½ oz/2 cups) roughly shredded cooked
  boneless, skinless chicken breast
250 g (9 oz) mixed cherry tomatoes, halved
200 g (7 oz) bocconcini (fresh baby mozzarella cheese),
  torn into chunks
basil leaves, shredded, to serve

TIP: For extra flavour,
sprinkle the pizzas with
dried red chilli flakes or
dried oregano before baking.

1 Cook the broccoli in a large saucepan of lightly salted boiling water for 1–2 minutes or until bright green and just tender. Refresh under cold running water then drain well.
2 Preheat oven to 230°C (450°F/Gas 8). Place two large, heavy pizza or baking trays in the oven to heat.
3 Cut the dough into four even portions and shape each into a ball. Press each ball to flatten, then use a lightly floured rolling pin to roll out each ball on a piece of non-stick baking paper to a 25 cm (10 in) round.

4 Spread the bases evenly with the tomato paste. Top with the shredded chicken, tomato halves, broccoli and bocconcini.
5 Remove the trays from the oven one at a time to keep them as hot as possible and carefully slide one pizza (still on the baking paper) onto each tray. Bake for 10 minutes, swapping the trays around halfway through cooking, or until the bases are crisp and golden. Bake the remaining two pizzas. Serve the pizzas immediately, sprinkled with the basil.

Cheats

Eggplant, semi-dried tomato & olive pizza

Preparation time: 10 minutes
Cooking time: 10–12 minutes
Makes: two 20 x 29 cm (8 x 11½ in) rectangle pizzas (serves 4)

2 x 300 g (10½ oz) (20 x 29 cm) (8 x 11½ in)
  bought rectangle pizza bases
125 ml (4 fl oz/½ cup) tomato passata (puréed tomatoes)
100 g (3½ oz) thinly sliced hot salami
200 g (7 oz) deli-bought chargrilled sliced eggplant (aubergine)
200 g (7 oz) bocconcini (fresh baby mozzarella cheese),
  torn into chunks
105 g (3½ oz/½ cup) semi-dried (sun-blushed) tomatoes, sliced
75 g (2¾ oz/½ cup) pitted kalamata olives
small basil leaves, to serve

1 Preheat oven to 220°C (425°F/Gas 7). Place two large, heavy baking trays in the oven to heat.
2 Spread each pizza base evenly with the tomato passata. Top with the salami, eggplant, bocconcini, tomato and olives.
3 Remove the trays from the oven one at a time to keep them as hot as possible and carefully place one pizza on each tray. Bake for 10–12 minutes, swapping the trays around halfway through cooking, or until the bases are crisp and golden.
4 Serve immediately, sprinkled with the basil.

Spicy smoked chicken, tomato & spinach pizza

Preparation time: 15 minutes
Cooking time: 10 minutes
Makes: four oval pizzas (serves 4)

80 ml (2½ fl oz/⅓ cup) tomato passata
  (puréed tomatoes)
¼ teaspoon dried red chilli flakes
4 x 70 g (2½ oz) bought naan bread (see tip)
200 g (7 oz) smoked chicken breast fillet, thinly sliced
125 g (4½ oz) marinated artichoke hearts, drained,
  halved lengthways
2 roma (plum) tomatoes, seeded, diced
1 small red onion, thinly sliced
125 g (4½ oz/1 cup, loosely packed) coarsely grated
  mozzarella cheese
40 g (1½ oz) baby spinach leaves, to serve

1 Preheat oven to 230°C (450°F/Gas 8). Place two large, heavy baking trays in the oven to heat.
2 Combine the tomato passata and chilli flakes in a bowl. Spread the naan breads evenly with the passata. Top with the chicken, artichokes, tomato, onion and mozzarella.
3 Remove the trays from the oven one at a time to keep them as hot as possible and carefully place two pizzas onto each tray. Bake for 10 minutes, swapping the trays around halfway through cooking, or until the bases are golden. Serve immediately, topped with the spinach.

TIP: You can use small pitta bread instead of the naan bread.

Tuna, tomato & chilli pizza

Preparation time: 10 minutes
Cooking time: 20 minutes
Makes: four 24 cm (9½ in) round pizzas (serves 4)

> four 24 cm (9½ in) bought thin round pizza bases
> 160 ml (5¼ fl oz/⅔ cup) tomato passata
>   (puréed tomatoes) or bought pizza sauce
> 220 g (7¾ oz) fresh buffalo mozzarella cheese, thinly sliced
> 2 garlic cloves, thinly sliced
> 425 g (15 oz) tin tuna in oil
> 2 small vine-ripened tomatoes, roughly chopped
> 2 teaspoons dried red chilli flakes
> 2 tablespoons coarsely chopped flat-leaf (Italian)
>   parsley, to serve

1 Preheat oven to 200°C (400°F/Gas 6).
2 Place each pizza on a piece of non-stick baking paper. Spread the pizzas evenly with the tomato passata, then top with the mozzarella and garlic. Drain the tuna in a sieve over a bowl to catch the oil. Break the tuna into large chunks and scatter over the pizzas with the tomato. Sprinkle with the chilli and drizzle each evenly with the reserved tuna oil. Season with salt.
3 Carefully slide two of the pizzas onto two separate large, heavy pizza or baking trays. Bake for 10 minutes, swapping the trays around halfway through cooking, or until golden. Bake the remaining two pizzas. Serve immediately, sprinkled with the parsley.

Chicken, vegetable & pesto pizza

Preparation time: 10 minutes
Cooking time: 15 minutes
Makes: two 20 x 30 cm (8 x 12 in) rectangle pizzas (serves 4)

> two 20 x 30 cm (8 x 12 in) bought rectangle thick pizza bases
> 125 ml (4 fl oz/½ cup) tomato passata (puréed tomatoes)
>   or bought pizza sauce
> 125 g (4½ oz/1 cup, loosely packed) coarsely grated mozzarella cheese
> 150 g (5½ oz) barbecue chicken meat, coarsely shredded
> 280 g (10 oz) jar mixed chargrilled vegetables in oil, drained
> 100 g (3½ oz/⅔ cup) crumbled feta cheese
> 2 tablespoons bought pesto

1 Preheat oven to 200°C (400°F/Gas 6). Place two large, heavy baking trays in the oven to heat.
2 Place each pizza on a piece of non-stick baking paper. Spread the pizzas evenly with the tomato passata, top with the mozzarella, chicken, chargrilled vegetables and feta, and then dollop the pesto over.
3 Remove the trays from the oven one at a time to keep them as hot as possible and carefully slide one pizza (still on the baking paper) onto each tray. Bake for 15 minutes, swapping the trays around halfway through cooking, or until the bases are crisp and golden. Serve immediately.

Artichoke, olive & thyme pizza

Preparation time: 15 minutes
Cooking time: 16 minutes
Makes: four large round pizzas (serves 4)

> 4 large round Lebanese breads
> 280 g (10 oz) jar marinated artichoke hearts, drained
> 160 ml (5¼ fl oz/⅔ cup) tomato passata (puréed tomatoes)
>   or bought pizza sauce
> 105 g (3½ oz/¾ cup, loosely packed) coarsely grated mozzarella cheese
> 110 g (3¾ oz/⅔ cup) pitted kalamata olives, halved
> 120 g (4¼ oz) goat's cheese, thickly sliced
> 2 tablespoons thyme leaves

1 Preheat oven to 200°C (400°F/Gas 6).

2 Place each Lebanese bread on a piece of non-stick baking paper. Cut the artichoke hearts into 2 cm (¾ in) wedges. Spread the breads evenly with the tomato passata, then top with half the mozzarella, the artichokes, olives, goat's cheese and thyme. Top with the remaining mozzarella. Season with salt.

3 Carefully slide two pizzas onto two separate large, heavy pizza or baking trays. Bake for 8 minutes, swapping the trays around halfway through cooking, or until the bases are crisp and golden. Bake the remaining two pizzas. Serve immediately.

Hot & fiery white bean, salami & ricotta pizza

Preparation time: 10 minutes
Cooking time: 20 minutes
Makes: four 30 cm (12 in) round pizzas (serves 4–8)

> four 30 cm (12 in) bought thick, sauced (tomato)
>   round pizza bases
> 230 g (8 oz/1 cup) firm, fresh ricotta cheese
> 2 teaspoons dried red chilli flakes, or to taste
> 400 g (14 oz) tin cannellini beans, rinsed, drained
> 225 g (8 oz) hot Spanish-style salami, thinly sliced
> 200 g (7 oz/2 cups, loosely packed) coarsely grated
>   gruyère cheese
> ½ cup oregano leaves

1 Preheat oven to 220°C (425°F/Gas 7). Place two large, heavy pizza or baking trays in the oven to heat.
2 Place each pizza base on a piece of non-stick baking paper. Spread the pizzas with the ricotta and sprinkle with the chilli flakes, then top with the cannellini beans, salami and gruyère and sprinkle with half the oregano.
3 Remove the trays from the oven one at a time to keep them as hot as possible and carefully slide one pizza (still on the baking paper) onto each tray. Bake for 10 minutes, swapping the trays halfway through cooking, or until the bases are crisp and golden. Bake the remaining two pizzas.
4 Serve immediately, sprinkled with the remaining oregano.

TIP: If you want less 'heat' in your pizzas, substitute mild salami for the hot Spanish-style salami or reduce the quantity of chilli flakes.

Sausage & semi-dried tomato pizza

Preparation time: 10 minutes
Cooking time: 12 minutes
Makes: four 15 x 21 cm (6 x 8¼ in) rectangle pizzas (serves 4)

two 21 x 30 cm (8¼ x 12 in) bought rectangle garlic and
  herb pizza bases, halved crossways
160 ml (5¼ fl oz/⅔ cup) tomato passata (puréed tomatoes)
260 g (9¼ oz) coarsely grated mozzarella cheese
105 g (3½ oz/½ cup) semi-dried (sun-blushed) tomatoes
90 g (3¼ oz) chargrilled capsicum (pepper), sliced
4 thin pork sausages (about 350 g/12 oz), skins removed, crumbled
60 g (2¼ oz) baby rocket (arugula)

1 Preheat oven to 220°C (425°F/Gas 7). Place two large, heavy baking trays in the oven to heat.
2 Place each pizza on a piece of non-stick baking paper. Spread the pizzas evenly with the tomato passata, leaving a small border, then top with the mozzarella, tomatoes, capsicum and crumbled sausage.
3 Remove the trays from the oven one at a time to keep them as hot as possible and carefully slide two pizzas (still on the baking paper) onto each tray. Bake for 12 minutes, swapping the trays around halfway through cooking, or until golden and the sausage is cooked.
4 Serve the pizzas immediately, topped with the rocket and seasoned with freshly ground black pepper.

Ham, olive & artichoke pizza

Preparation time: 10 minutes
Cooking time: 15 minutes
Makes: six small round pizzas (serves 6 as a starter)

6 pitta breads
200 g (7 oz) coarsely grated edam cheese
240 g (8¾ oz) shaved leg ham
100 g (3½ oz) stuffed green olives, halved
6 marinated artichoke hearts, drained, sliced crossways
  into thirds
¼ cup flat-leaf (Italian) parsley leaves (see tip)

1 Preheat oven to 220°C (425°F/Gas 7). Place two large, heavy baking trays in the oven to heat.
2 Top the pitta breads with two-thirds of the edam, then the ham, olives and artichokes, then sprinkle with the remaining edam.
3 Remove the trays from the oven one at a time to keep them as hot as possible and carefully place three pizzas on each tray. Bake for 15 minutes, swapping the trays halfway through cooking, or until the bases are crisp and golden.
4 Serve the pizzas immediately, sprinkled with the parsley.

TIP: You can use oregano leaves instead of the parsley.

Vegetarian

Leek, blue cheese & rosemary pizza

Preparation time: 20 minutes
Cooking time: 40 minutes
Makes: four 24 cm (9½ in) round pizzas (serves 4)

> 3 large leeks (about 1.5 kg/3 lb 5 oz), white part
>   only, trimmed, washed well
> 60 ml (2 fl oz/¼ cup) olive oil
> 2 rosemary sprigs
> 1 quantity pizza dough (see page 118)
> 200 g (7 oz) firm blue cheese, coarsely crumbled
> 50 g (1¾ oz/⅓ cup) pine nuts

1 Cut the leeks into 1 cm (½ in) thick rounds. Heat the olive oil in a large saucepan over medium heat. Add the leeks and 1 rosemary sprig, cover and cook, stirring occasionally, for 15 minutes or until the leeks are tender. Discard the rosemary sprig. Transfer the leeks to a colander and drain well, pressing down on the leeks gently to expel as much liquid as possible. Cool slightly.

2 Preheat oven to 220°C (425°F/Gas 7). Place two large, heavy pizza or baking trays in the oven to heat.

3 Cut the dough into four even portions and shape each into a ball. Press each ball to flatten, then use a lightly floured rolling pin to roll out each ball on a piece of non-stick baking paper to a 24 cm (9½ in) round.

4 Spread the bases evenly with the leeks, then top with the blue cheese.

5 Remove the trays from the oven one at a time to keep them as hot as possible and carefully slide one pizza (still on the baking paper) onto each tray. Bake for 7 minutes. Remove the pizzas from the oven and sprinkle them with half the pine nuts. Return the pizzas to the oven, swapping the trays around, and bake for another 5 minutes or until the pizza bases are crisp and golden and the cheese is bubbling. Repeat with the remaining two pizzas and pine nuts. Serve immediately, sprinkled with the leaves from the remaining rosemary sprig.

Chickpea & pumpkin pizza

Preparation time: 25 minutes
Cooking time: 35 minutes
Makes: six 16 cm (6¼ in) round pizzas (serves 6 as a starter or snack)

500 g (1 lb 2 oz) butternut pumpkin (squash), peeled, seeded
60 ml (2 fl oz/¼ cup) olive oil
400 g (14 oz) tin chickpeas, rinsed, drained
1 quantity pizza sauce (see page 120)
1 tablespoon chopped sage leaves
1 quantity pizza dough (see page 118)
250 g (9 oz) coarsely grated Swiss cheese
24 sage leaves

1 Preheat oven to 180°C (350°F/Gas 4). Cut the pumpkin into wedges about 4 cm (1½ in) thick then cut widthways into slices about 7 mm (⅜ in) thick. Place in a large roasting dish, drizzle with the olive oil then roast for 15 minutes or until tender. Set aside.
2 Increase the oven to 220°C (425°F/Gas 7). Place three large, heavy pizza or baking trays in the oven to heat.
3 Place the chickpeas in a bowl and use a fork to coarsely crush. Add the pizza sauce and the chopped sage and stir to combine.
4 Cut the dough into six even portions and shape each into a ball. Press each ball to flatten, then use a lightly floured rolling pin to roll out each ball on a piece of non-stick baking paper to a 16 cm (6¼ in) round.
5 Spread the pizzas evenly with the chickpea mixture, then sprinkle with the cheese. Top with the roasted pumpkin and the sage leaves.
6 Remove the trays from the oven one at a time to keep them as hot as possible and carefully slide two pizzas (still on the baking paper) onto each tray. Bake for 15–20 minutes, swapping the trays around halfway through cooking, or until the bases are crisp and golden and the cheese is bubbling. Serve immediately.

Lentil lamachun

Preparation time: 20 minutes
Cooking time: 26 minutes
Makes: six pizzas (serves 6)

> 500 g ripe roma (plum) tomatoes
> 2½ tablespoons olive oil, plus extra, for greasing
> 1 brown onion, finely chopped
> 2 garlic cloves, crushed
> 1½ tablespoons tomato paste (concentrated purée)
> 1 teaspoon sweet paprika
> 1 teaspoon ground allspice
> ¼ teaspoon cayenne pepper, or to taste (optional)
> 2 x 400 g (14 oz) tins brown lentils, rinsed, drained
> 1 bunch coriander (cilantro), chopped, plus extra sprigs, to garnish
> 1 quantity wholemeal pizza dough (see page 118)
> 125 g (4½ oz) feta cheese, coarsely crumbled

1 Cut the tomatoes into quarters lengthways and remove the seeds. Chop the tomatoes into 5 mm (¼ in) pieces.

2 Heat the olive oil in a large heavy-based saucepan over medium heat. Cook the onion and garlic, stirring often, for 3–4 minutes or until starting to soften. Add the tomato paste and spices then cook, stirring constantly, for 1–2 minutes or until fragrant. Stir in the tomato and lentils then remove from the heat and cool slightly. Stir in the coriander.

3 Preheat oven to 220°C (425°F/Gas 7). Lightly grease two large, heavy baking trays with olive oil. Cut the dough into six even portions and shape each into a ball. Press each ball to flatten, then use a lightly floured rolling pin to roll out each ball on a lightly floured surface to a 15 x 24 cm (6 x 9½ in) oval.

4 Divide the cooled lentil mixture among the pizzas, piling it down the centre and leaving a 2.5 cm (1 in) border. Scatter with the feta. Bring the edges up to contain the filling, pinching the ends to create torpedo-shaped pizzas.

5 Carefully place the pizzas on the trays. Bake for 20 minutes, swapping the trays around halfway through cooking, or until crisp and golden. Serve warm or at room temperature, garnished with extra coriander.

Mixed mushroom & asparagus pizza

Preparation time: 10 minutes (+ cooling time)
Cooking time: 45 minutes
Makes: four 25 cm (10 in) square pizzas (serves 4)

8 garlic cloves, unpeeled
1 quantity roasted tomato pizza sauce (see page 120)
2 tablespoons olive oil
150 g (5½ oz) small button mushrooms
200 g (7 oz) Swiss brown mushrooms, thickly sliced
1 bunch asparagus (about 180 g/6¼ oz)
1 quantity pizza dough (see page 118)
240 g (8¾ oz) fresh buffalo mozzarella cheese, thinly sliced

1 Roast the garlic at the same time as you roast the tomatoes for the roasted tomato pizza sauce. Place the garlic on a double layer of foil, drizzle with 2 teaspoons of the olive oil and seal. Bake for 25 minutes or until soft. Cool slightly and remove from the skins.

2 Cut half of the button mushrooms in half. Heat a large non-stick frying pan over high heat and add the remaining olive oil. Add all the button and swiss brown mushrooms, season with salt and freshly ground black pepper and cook for 3–4 minutes, stirring occasionally, or until just tender. Transfer to a plate to cool.

3 Preheat oven to 220°C (425°F/Gas 7). Place two large, heavy baking trays in the oven to heat.

4 Trim the asparagus and cut each spear into three pieces. Cook the asparagus in salted boiling water for 1 minute or until par-cooked. Refresh in a bowl of iced water. Drain and set aside.

5 Cut the dough into four even portions and shape each into a ball. Press each ball to flatten, then use a lightly floured rolling pin to roll out each ball on a piece of non-stick baking paper to a 25 cm (10 in) square.

6 Spread the pizzas evenly with the pizza sauce, leaving a small border, then top with half the mozzarella, the mushrooms, garlic, asparagus and then the remaining mozzarella.

7 Remove the trays from the oven one at a time to keep them as hot as possible and carefully slide one pizza (still on the baking paper) onto each tray. Bake for 10 minutes, swapping the trays around halfway through cooking. Bake the remaining two pizzas. Serve immediately.

Eggplant & tomato pizza

Preparation time: 20 minutes
Cooking time: 45 minutes
Makes: four 16 x 30 cm (6¼ x 12 in) rectangle pizzas (serves 4)

125 ml (4 fl oz/½ cup) extra virgin olive oil
1 large eggplant (aubergine) (about 500 g/1 lb 2 oz), cut into 5 mm (¼ in) thick slices
2 red onions, each cut into 8 wedges
1 quantity pizza dough (see page 118)
300 g (10½ oz) fresh buffalo mozzarella cheese, thinly sliced
4 small ripe tomatoes, thinly sliced
80 g (2¾ oz) finely grated smoked cheddar cheese (see tip)
4 garlic cloves, finely chopped
40 g (1½ oz/⅔ cup, lightly packed) fresh breadcrumbs, made from day-old bread

TIP: If you can't find smoked cheddar use any other firm smoked cheese.

1 Heat 80 ml (2½ fl oz/⅓ cup) of the olive oil in a large frying pan over medium–high heat and cook the eggplant in batches for 2 minutes each side or until just browned. Drain on paper towel.

2 Heat the remaining oil in the same pan over medium heat and cook the onion, stirring occasionally, for 10 minutes, or until lightly browned.

3 Preheat oven to 230°C (450°F/Gas 8). Place two large, heavy baking trays in the oven to heat.

4 Cut the dough into four even portions and shape each into a ball. Press each ball to flatten, then use a lightly floured rolling pin to roll out each ball on a piece of non-stick baking paper to a 16 x 30 cm (6¼ x 12 in) rectangle. Make a border, pressing with your fingertips 2 cm (¾ in) from the edge.

5 Top the pizzas with the mozzarella, eggplant, tomato and onion. Sprinkle with the smoke cheddar, garlic and breadcrumbs and season with salt and freshly ground black pepper.

6 Remove the trays from the oven one at a time to keep them as hot as possible and carefully slide one pizza (still on the baking paper) onto each tray. Bake for 10 minutes, swapping the trays around halfway through cooking, or until the bases are crisp and golden. Bake the remaining two pizzas. Serve immediately.

Tomato & ricotta pizza with olive tapenade

Preparation time: 15 minutes
Cooking time: 10 minutes
Makes: two 25 cm (10 in) round pizzas (serves 4)

1 quantity pizza dough (see page 118)
80 ml (2½ fl oz/⅓ cup) pizza sauce (see page 120)
2 tablespoons olive tapenade (see page 123)
160 g (5¾ oz) firm, fresh ricotta cheese
160 g (5¾ oz) mixed cherry and teardrop tomatoes, halved

1 Preheat oven to 220°C (425°F/Gas 7). Place two large, heavy pizza or baking trays in the oven to heat.
2 Cut the dough into two even portions and shape each into a ball. Press each ball to flatten, then use a lightly floured rolling pin to roll out each ball on a piece of non-stick baking paper to a 25 cm (10 in) round. Make a border, pressing with your fingertips 2 cm (¾ in) from the edge.
3 Spread the pizzas evenly with the pizza sauce and dollop with the tapenade. Crumble over the ricotta, arrange the tomato halves on top and season with sea salt and freshly ground black pepper.
4 Remove the trays from the oven one at a time to keep them as hot as possible and carefully slide one pizza (still on the baking paper) onto each tray. Bake for 10 minutes, swapping the trays around halfway through cooking, or until the bases are golden and cooked through. Serve immediately.

Salsa verde pizza

Preparation time: 10 minutes
Cooking time: 20 minutes
Makes: four 25 cm (10 in) round pizzas (serves 4)

> 1 quantity pizza dough (see page 118)
> 125 ml (4 fl oz/½ cup) extra virgin olive oil
> 240 g (8 ¾ oz) bocconcini (fresh baby mozzarella cheese),
>   thinly sliced, drained on paper towel
> ¾ cup finely chopped flat-leaf (Italian) parsley
> 2 tablespoons salted baby capers, rinsed, drained
> 4 garlic cloves, chopped
> 40 g (1½ oz) rocket (arugula)

1 Preheat oven to 230°C (450°F/Gas 8). Place two large, heavy pizza or baking trays in the oven to heat.

2 Cut the dough into four even portions and shape each into a ball. Press each ball to flatten, then use a lightly floured rolling pin to roll out each ball on a piece of non-stick baking paper to a 25 cm (10 in) round.

3 Brush the pizzas with half the olive oil, then top with half the bocconcini, leaving a small border. Sprinkle over the parsley, capers and garlic. Top with the remaining bocconcini.

4 Remove the trays from the oven one at a time to keep them as hot as possible and carefully slide one pizza (still on the baking paper) onto each tray. Bake for 8–10 minutes, swapping the trays around halfway through cooking, or until the bases are crisp and golden. Bake the remaining two pizzas. Serve the pizzas immediately, topped with the rocket and drizzled with the remaining olive oil.

Silverbeet & raisin calzone

Preparation time: 25 minutes
Cooking time: 45 minutes
Makes: six calzone (serves 6)

1 kg (2 lb 4 oz) silverbeet (Swiss chard) (about 1 large bunch)
60 ml (2 fl oz/¼ cup) olive oil, plus extra, for greasing
1 large brown onion, chopped
3 garlic cloves, finely chopped
75 g (2¾ oz/⅓ cup) pine nuts
60 g (2¼ oz/⅓ cup) raisins, coarsely chopped
2 tablespoons red wine vinegar
150 g (5½ oz/1½ cups, loosely packed) finely shredded parmesan cheese
1½ quantities pizza dough (see page 118)
lemon wedges, to serve

1 Wash the silverbeet leaves and shake dry. Remove the stems and reserve. Finely shred the leaves then set aside. Trim the ends of the stems and then finely chop the stems. Heat the oil in a very large saucepan over medium heat. Add the chopped stems, onion, garlic and pine nuts and cook, stirring often, for 10 minutes or until the vegetables are soft and the pine nuts are light golden. Add the silverbeet leaves, raisins and vinegar, increase the heat to high then cook, stirring often, for 5–6 minutes or until the leaves are wilted. Cook for 2–3 minutes or until the excess liquid evaporates (the mixture should not be wet). Transfer to a bowl and cool slightly. Stir through the parmesan and season with salt and freshly ground black pepper.

2 Preheat oven to 220°C (425°F/Gas 7). Lightly grease two large, heavy baking trays.

3 Cut the dough into six even portions and shape each into a ball. Press each ball to flatten, then use a lightly floured rolling pin to roll out each ball on a lightly floured surface to a 23 cm (9 in) round.

4 Divide the silverbeet mixture among the dough rounds, piling it evenly over one half only and leaving a 1.5 cm (⅝ in) border around the edges. Use a pastry brush or your fingertips to lightly brush the borders with water. Fold the uncovered half of each dough round up and over the filling, then press the edges together to seal well.

5 Carefully transfer the calzone to the trays, bending them slightly from the middle to make a half-moon shape. Bake for 25 minutes, swapping the trays around halfway through cooking, or until the crusts are golden and cooked through. Serve immediately with lemon wedges.

Roasted eggplant & garlic pizza

Preparation time: 25 minutes (+ cooling time)
Cooking time: 45 minutes
Makes: four 25 cm (10 in) round pizzas (serves 4)

8 garlic cloves, unpeeled
60 ml (2 fl oz/¼ cup) olive oil
1 eggplant (aubergine) (about 450 g/1 lb)
1 quantity wholemeal pizza dough (see page 118)
1 quantity pizza sauce (see page 120)
200 g (7 oz) fresh buffalo mozzarella cheese, thinly sliced
⅓ cup oregano leaves
105 g (3½ oz/½ cup) mint & chilli pesto (see page 122)
¼ cup flat-leaf (Italian) parsley leaves

1 Preheat oven to 200°C (400°F/Gas 6). Line a baking tray with non-stick baking paper.
2 Place the garlic on a double layer of foil, drizzle with 2 teaspoons of the olive oil and seal. Cut the eggplant into 2 cm (¾ in) chunks and place in a bowl with the remaining olive oil. Season with salt and toss to combine. Spread the eggplant on the lined tray. Place the garlic parcel on the tray with the eggplant. Roast for 25 minutes or until the eggplant is just tender and starting to colour. Set aside to cool. Remove the garlic from the skins.
3 Increase the oven to 220°C (425°F/Gas 7). Place two large, heavy pizza or baking trays in the oven to heat.
4 Cut the dough into four even portions and shape each into a ball. Press each ball to flatten, then use a lightly floured rolling pin to roll out each ball on a piece of non-stick baking paper to a 25 cm (10 in) round.
5 Spread the pizzas evenly with the pizza sauce, then top with half the mozzarella, the eggplant, garlic, oregano and the remaining mozzarella.
6 Remove the trays from the oven one at a time to keep them as hot as possible and carefully slide one pizza (still on the baking paper) onto each tray. Bake for 10 minutes, swapping the trays around halfway through cooking, or until the bases are crisp and golden. Bake the remaining two pizzas. Serve the pizzas immediately, topped with the mint & chilli pesto and sprinkled with the parsley.

Mini balsamic onion & goat's cheese pizzas

Preparation time: 35 minutes (+ cooling time)
Cooking time: 1 hour 5 minutes
Makes: 46 mini round pizzas

80 ml (2½ fl oz/⅓ cup) olive oil
1.5 kg (3 lb 5 oz) brown onions, halved lengthways, thinly sliced
3 teaspoons caster (superfine) sugar
2 tablespoons balsamic vinegar
1 quantity parmesan pizza dough (see page 118), made using
  1 tablespoon dried mint added to the flour mixture
300 g (10½ oz) pitted black olives, halved lengthways
220 g (7¾ oz) soft goat's cheese, crumbled
½ cup firmly packed small mint leaves, to garnish

1 Heat the olive oil in a very large saucepan over medium heat and cook the onion, stirring often, for 35–40 minutes or until very soft and starting to caramelise. Add the sugar and vinegar then cook, stirring, for 5 minutes or until any excess liquid has evaporated. Season with salt and freshly ground black pepper. Set aside to cool.

2 Preheat oven to 230°C (450°F/Gas 8). Line four large, heavy baking trays with non-stick baking paper.

3 Take a small, walnut-sized portion of dough and roll out on a lightly floured surface to a 6 cm (2½ in) round. Repeat with the remaining dough to make another 45 bases. Place on the trays, leaving 2 cm (¾ in) between each.

4 Top the pizzas with the onion mixture, olives and goat's cheese.

5 Bake two trays of pizzas for 10 minutes, swapping the trays around halfway through cooking, or until the bases are crisp and golden. Bake the remaining trays of pizzas. Serve the pizzas immediately, garnished with the mint.

Basics

Pizza dough

Preparation time: 20 minutes (+ 1 hour proving time)
Makes: enough for four 25 cm (10 in) thin-based pizzas or two 25 cm (10 in) thick-based pizzas

> 400 g (14 oz/2⅔ cups) plain flour
> 14 g (½ oz/ 1 tablespoon) dried yeast
> 2 teaspoons sugar
> 1 teaspoon salt
> 250 ml (9 fl oz/1 cup) lukewarm water
> 3 teaspoons olive oil

1 Place the flour, yeast, sugar and salt in a bowl and make a well in the centre. Combine the water and olive oil and add to the flour mixture. Use a wooden spoon and then your hands to mix to a dough.
2 Turn onto a lightly floured surface and knead for 5 minutes or until smooth and elastic.
3 Place the dough in an oiled bowl and turn to coat lightly in the oil. Cover loosely with a clean, slightly damp tea towel (dish towel) or plastic wrap and set aside in a warm, draught-free place for 1 hour or until doubled in size.
4 Knock back the dough by punching your fist into the centre of the dough. Turn onto a lightly floured surface and knead for 2–3 minutes or until smooth and elastic. Use immediately as directed.

Variations:

Wholemeal pizza dough: Replace the plain flour with 400 g (14 oz/2⅔ cups) wholemeal flour and add an extra 50 ml (1½ fl oz) lukewarm water.
Gluten-free pizza dough: Replace the plain flour with 400 g (14 oz/2⅔ cups) gluten-free flour and add 1 extra tablespoon of lukewarm water.
Rosemary pizza dough: After kneading in step 2, add 2 teaspoons very finely chopped rosemary and knead for another 1 minute to incorporate.
Parmesan pizza dough: After kneading in step 2, add 40 g (1½ oz) finely grated parmesan cheese and knead for another 1 minute to incorporate.

TIPS:

- To reduce the proving time by about half, divide the pizza dough into portions (according to the number of pizzas you are going to make) before setting aside to prove.

- When cutting the pizza dough into portions, use a floured knife to make it easy and stick-free.

- Use good-quality, heavy pizza or baking trays to cook the pizzas—they will retain heat more effectively and help give you a crisp base.

- If possible, always preheat the pizza or baking trays in the oven so that the pizzas can go straight onto hot trays. Hot, good-quality trays will result in crisp bases—just be careful when transferring the pizzas onto them before baking.

- Roll out the pizzas on non-stick baking paper then use this to lift the pizzas onto the hot trays to avoid burning your fingers.

- You can use pizza stones to cook all the pizzas in this book to help achieve crisp bases. However, remember your pizzas will take less time to cook—usually 2–5 minutes less.

- Swapping the trays around about halfway through cooking will ensure that your pizzas cook evenly and will be ready at the same time.

Pizza sauce

Preparation time: 10 minutes
Cooking time: 25 minutes
Makes: 250 ml (9 fl oz/1 cup)

> 1 tablespoon olive oil
> ¼ brown onion, finely chopped
> 1 garlic clove, finely chopped
> 400 g (14 oz) tin whole tomatoes
> 5 basil leaves
> pinch of sugar, or to taste

1 Heat the oil in a small saucepan over low heat. Add the onion and garlic and cook, stirring occasionally, for 6 minutes or until softened.

2 Add the tomatoes and basil, then use a potato masher to crush the tomatoes. Simmer, stirring occasionally, for 15–18 minutes or until thickened. Taste and season with sugar, salt and freshly ground black pepper. Set aside to cool to room temperature.

Variations:

Roasted tomato pizza sauce: Halve 700 g (1 lb 9 oz) roma (plum) tomatoes. Place on a baking tray, cut sides up, drizzle with 1 tablespoon olive oil and sprinkle with the leaves from 4 thyme sprigs. Roast at 180°C (350°F/Gas 4) for 30–40 minutes or until lightly roasted. Follow recipe for pizza sauce above, using the roasted tomatoes instead of tinned tomatoes.

Tomato & chilli pizza sauce: Add 1 finely chopped small red chilli with the onion and garlic.

Herb pizza sauce: Stir 1 tablespoon finely snipped chives and 1 tablespoon finely chopped flat-leaf (Italian) parsley through the sauce at the end of cooking.

Clockwise from top: pizza sauce, olive tapenade and mint & chilli pesto.

Pesto

Preparation time: 10 minutes
Makes: 210 g (7½ oz/1 cup)

> 55 g (2 oz/1¾ cups) loosely packed basil leaves
> 1 garlic clove, finely chopped
> 50 g (1¾ oz/⅓ cup) finely grated parmesan cheese
> 40 g (1½ oz/¼ cup) pine nuts
> 125 ml (4 fl oz/½ cup) olive oil

1 Place the basil, garlic, parmesan and pine nuts in a food processor and pulse until roughly chopped.
2 With the motor running, gradually add the oil to combine. Season with salt and freshly ground black pepper.

Variations:

Rocket pesto: Replace the basil with 55 g (2 oz/1⅔ cups) wild rocket (arugula).
Mint & chilli pesto: Replace the basil with 20 g (¾ oz/1 cup, lightly packed) mint leaves and 10 g (¼ oz/½ cup, lightly packed) flat-leaf (Italian) parsley leaves. Add ½ long red chilli, seeded and chopped.

Olive tapenade

Preparation time: 10 minutes
Makes: 250 g (9 oz/1 cup)

> 205 g (7¼ oz/1⅓ cups) pitted kalamata olives
> 1 garlic clove, chopped
> 1 tablespoon salted baby capers, rinsed, drained
> 6 anchovy fillets, drained, chopped
> 15 g (½ oz/½ cup, firmly packed) flat-leaf (Italian) parsley leaves
> finely grated zest of ½ lemon
> 1 tablespoon lemon juice
> 80 ml (2½ fl oz/⅓ cup) extra virgin olive oil

1 Place the olives, garlic, capers, anchovies and parsley in a small food processor and pulse until coarsely chopped.
2 Stir through the lemon zest and juice and the olive oil. Season with salt and freshly ground black pepper.

Variations:

Green olive tapenade: Replace the kalamata olives with green olives. (Pitted unstuffed green olives are often hard to find so use a small knife to remove the flesh from 300 g (10½ oz) whole large green olives – you should have 200 g/7 oz flesh.)

Semi-dried tomato tapenade: Replace the kalamata olives with 200 g (7 oz) semi-dried tomatoes. Replace the parsley with the same amount of basil leaves.

Index

Published in 2011 by Murdoch Books Pty Limited

Murdoch Books Australia
Pier 8/9
23 Hickson Road
Millers Point NSW 2000
Phone: +61 (0) 2 8220 2000
Fax: +61 (0) 2 8220 2558
www.murdochbooks.com.au

Murdoch Books UK Limited
Erico House, 6th Floor
93–99 Upper Richmond Road
Putney, London SW15 2TG
Phone: +44 (0) 20 8785 5995
Fax: +44 (0) 20 8785 5985
www.murdochbooks.co.uk

Publisher: Kylie Walker
Food Development Editor: Anneka Manning
Project Editor: Laura Wilson
Editor: Melissa Penn
Designers: Alex Frampton and Tania Gomes
Cover design: Vivien Valk
Photographer: Michele Aboud
Stylist: Sarah de Nardi
Illustrator: Alex Frampton
Production: Renee Melbourne

Recipe development: Chrissy Freer, Sonia Greig, Leanne Kitchen and Kathy Snowball
Food preparation for photography: Nick Branbury and Grace Campbell

National Library of Australia Cataloguing-in-Publication Data
Title: Make Me: Pizza.
ISBN: 978-1-74266-326-5 (pbk.)
Notes: Includes index.
Subjects: Pizza.
Dewey Number: 641.8248
A catalogue record for this book is available from the British Library.

Printed by 1010 Printing International Limited, China

OVEN GUIDE: You may find cooking times vary depending on the oven you are using. For
fan-forced ovens, as a general rule, set the oven temperature to 20°C (35°F) lower than
indicated in the recipe.

On cover: Moroccan chicken pizza (page 76).